IMPROMTU

SOLO FOR TROMBONE AND PIANO

GEORG WILKENSCHILDT

ALLEGRO MODERATO

Copyright © 1969 by Wilhelm Hansen, Copenhagen   28.991

WILHELM HANSEN EDITION NR. 7174

GEORG WILKENSCHILDT

IMPROMTU

SOLO FOR TROMBONE AND PIANO

COMPOSED DECEMBER 1938 . REVISED EDITION FEBRUARY 1969

Norsk Musikforlag A/S
OSLO

AB Nordiska Musikförlaget
STOCKHOLM

WILHELM HANSEN MUSIK-FORLAG
KØBENHAVN

J. & W. Chester Ltd.
LONDON

Wilhelmiana Musikverlag
FRANKFURT A.M.

IMPROMTU

SOLO FOR TROMBONE AND PIANO

GEORG WILKENSCHILDT

WH-tryk, Copenhagen